Earth Basics
Minerals

by Rebecca Pettiford

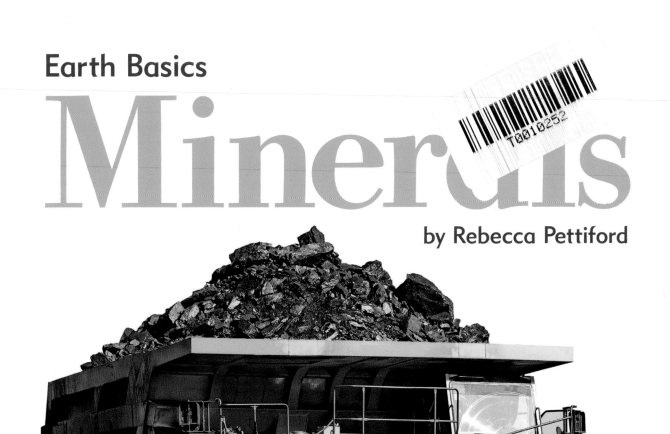

Bullfrog
Books

Ideas for Parents and Teachers

Bullfrog Books let children practice reading informational text at the earliest reading levels. Repetition, familiar words, and photo labels support early readers.

Before Reading

- Discuss the cover photo. What does it tell them?

- Look at the picture glossary together. Read and discuss the words.

Read the Book

- "Walk" through the book and look at the photos. Let the child ask questions. Point out the photo labels.

- Read the book to the child, or have him or her read independently.

After Reading

- Prompt the child to think more. Ask: Did you know minerals are in so many foods? Did you eat any foods with calcium or iron in them today?

Bullfrog Books are published by Jump!
5357 Penn Avenue South
Minneapolis, MN 55419
www.jumplibrary.com

Library of Congress Cataloging-in-Publication Data

Names: Pettiford, Rebecca, author.
Title: Minerals / by Rebecca Pettiford.
Description: Minneapolis, MN: Jump!, Inc., [2024]
Series: Earth basics | Includes index.
Audience: Ages 5–8
Identifiers: LCCN 2022043066 (print)
LCCN 2022043067 (ebook)
ISBN 9798885244398 (hardcover)
ISBN 9798885244404 (paperback)
ISBN 9798885244411 (ebook)
Subjects: LCSH: Minerals—Juvenile literature.
Classification: LCC QE365.2 .P4873 2024 (print)
LCC QE365.2 (ebook)
DDC 549—dc23/eng20230111
LC record available at https://lccn.loc.gov/2022043066
LC ebook record available at https://lccn.loc.gov/2022043067

Editor: Katie Chanez
Designer: Emma Almgren-Bersie

Photo Credits: Obradovic/iStock, cover; Parilov/Shutterstock, 1; Sebastian Janicki/Shutterstock, 3, 24; Igor_Profe/iStock, 4; Nora Yusuf/Shutterstock, 5; Fotystory/Shutterstock, 6–7; Ioan Panaite/Shutterstock, 8; mikulas1/iStock, 8–9, 23bl; Bjoern Wylezich/Shutterstock, 10 (left), 23tr; DmitrySt/Shutterstock, 10 (right), 23br; Karimpard/iStock, 11; Clovera/iStock, 12–13; Prostock-studio/Shutterstock, 14–15; Plateresca/Shutterstock, 16–17, 23tm; Anton Starikov/Shutterstock, 18, 23tl; Makistock/Shutterstock, 19; TadejZupancic/iStock, 20–21; phoelixDE/Shutterstock, 22tl; Danny Smythe/Shutterstock, 22tr; Arunsri Futemwong/Shutterstock, 22 (middle); Kenishirotie/Shutterstock, 22bl; donatas1205/Shutterstock, 22br; Oh suti/Shutterstock, 23bm.

Printed in the United States of America at Corporate Graphics in North Mankato, Minnesota.

Table of Contents

Rocks and Rings

Jack has a rock.

It is made of minerals.

**Minerals are hard substances.
They form on Earth.**

5

They are in sand and soil.
They are in water.

We dig mines.
They are below
the ground.
There, we dig up
minerals.

mineral

mine

gold

diamond

There are many kinds.
Gold is one.
Diamonds are another.

They make a ring.
Pretty!

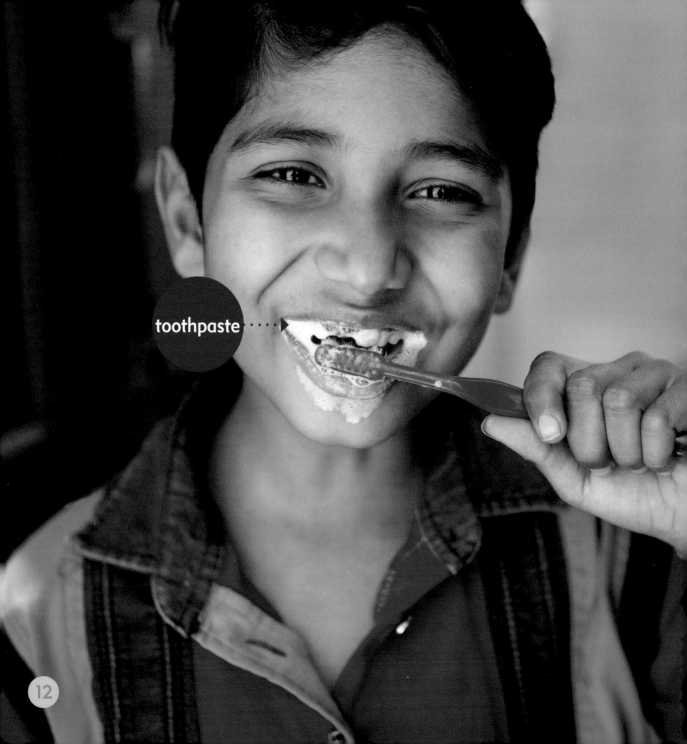

toothpaste

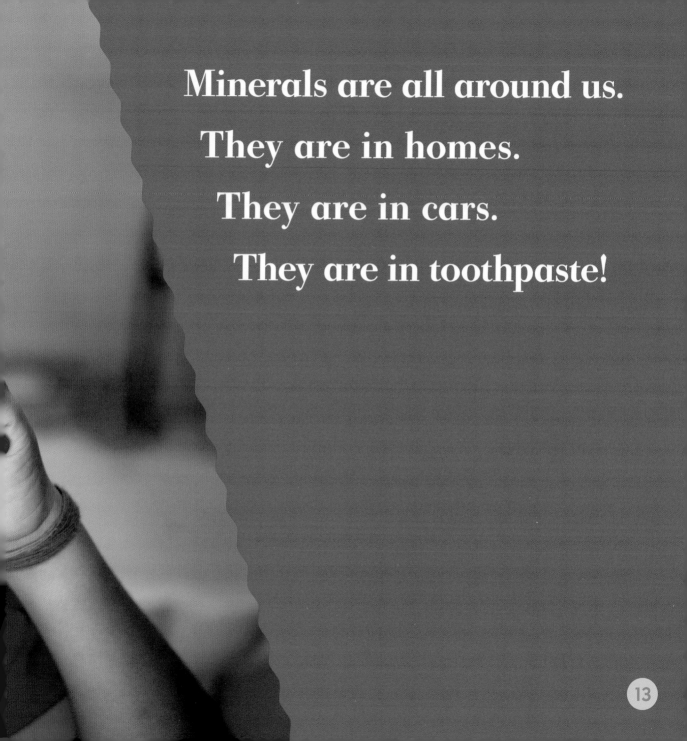

Minerals are all around us.

They are in homes.

They are in cars.

They are in toothpaste!

They are not alive.
But they help us live.
How?
They are in foods!

Iron is in meat.

It is in beans, too.

Calcium is in nuts.

almonds

It is in milk, too.

Minerals make us strong!

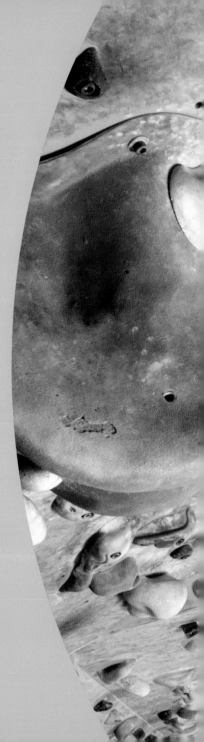

Minerals at Home

Minerals are things on Earth that do not come from animals or plants. What minerals are in items around your home? Take a look!

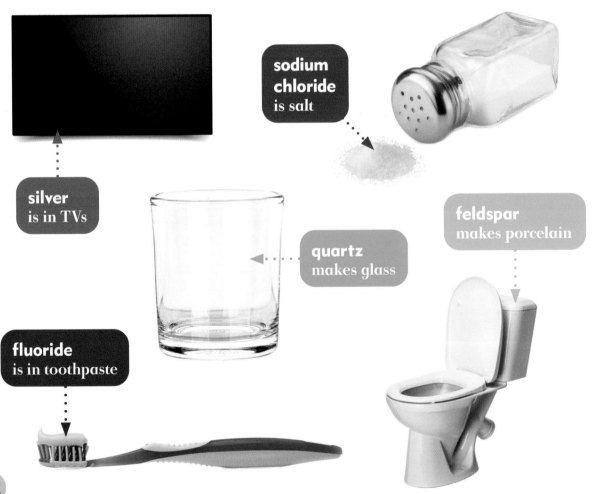

sodium chloride is salt

silver is in TVs

feldspar makes porcelain

quartz makes glass

fluoride is in toothpaste

Picture Glossary

calcium
A mineral in foods like milk and nuts.

iron
A mineral in foods like meat and beans.

minerals
Hard substances found on Earth that do not come from animals or plants.

mines
Places where people dig up minerals from below the ground.

soil
The top layer of Earth in which plants grow.

substances
Things that have weight and take up space.

Index

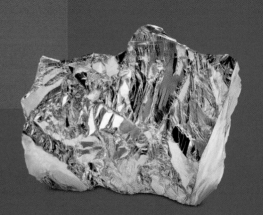

To Learn More

Finding more information is as easy as 1, 2, 3.

❶ Go to www.factsurfer.com

❷ Enter "minerals" into the search box.

❸ Choose your book to see a list of websites.